PRINCEWILL LAGANG

Cultural Perspectives on Marriage and Love

First published by PRINCEWILL LAGANG 2023

Copyright © 2023 by Princewill Lagang

All rights reserved. No part of this publication may be reproduced, stored or transmitted in any form or by any means, electronic, mechanical, photocopying, recording, scanning, or otherwise without written permission from the publisher. It is illegal to copy this book, post it to a website, or distribute it by any other means without permission.

Princewill Lagang asserts the moral right to be identified as the author of this work.

First edition

This book was professionally typeset on Reedsy.
Find out more at reedsy.com

Contents

1. Introduction — 1
2. Love Across Cultures — 4
3. Traditional Marriage Customs — 7
4. Arranged Marriages — 10
5. Family and Community Involvement — 13
6. Gender Roles and Expectations — 16
7. Love and Religion — 19
8. Celebrating Milestones and Anniversaries — 22
9. Relationship Dynamics in Changing Times — 25
10. Cross-Cultural Relationships — 28
11. Conflict Resolution Across Cultures — 31
12. Celebrating Diversity and Unity — 34

1

Introduction

In a world characterized by an ever-increasing interconnectedness, the exploration of diverse cultural perspectives on love and marriage takes on a profound significance. This book embarks on a journey that delves into the intricate interplay between culture and the fundamental human experiences of love and marriage. By examining these experiences through various cultural lenses, we aim to unravel the multifaceted tapestry that shapes human relationships around the globe.

1.1 The Focus of the Book

At the heart of this book lies an exploration of the diverse and nuanced ways in which different cultures perceive, experience, and navigate the realms of love and marriage. We endeavor to shed light on the cultural norms, values, and traditions that influence the formation and sustenance of romantic partnerships across societies. By examining both similarities and distinctions, we hope to illuminate universal threads while celebrating the richness of human diversity.

1.2 Understanding Culture's Influence

The intricate ways in which culture molds our perceptions and behaviors are particularly evident in the domains of love and marriage. Cultural norms dictate not only the acceptable expressions of affection but also the rituals and practices associated with courtship, union, and familial ties. A profound understanding of these influences is crucial in unraveling the complexities of human relationships. It enables us to appreciate how love and marriage are not solely personal matters but rather deeply embedded within broader cultural contexts.

1.3 Significance of the Exploration

Why is it essential to embark on a journey that examines love and marriage through the lens of culture? The answer lies in the recognition that these aspects of human life are not confined to individual experiences; they are inherently shaped by historical, social, and cultural factors. By immersing ourselves in diverse cultural perspectives, we gain a deeper appreciation for the intricate interplay between tradition and modernity, individual desires and communal expectations. This exploration equips us with the tools to foster cross-cultural empathy and understanding, which are paramount in our increasingly globalized world.

1.4 Structure of the Book

This book is structured to provide a comprehensive examination of the interconnections between culture, love, and marriage. Each subsequent chapter focuses on a specific cultural context, delving into its historical background, societal norms, and unique narratives surrounding love and marriage. By weaving together these varied accounts, we hope to construct a holistic tapestry that encapsulates the global diversity of human relationships.

In conclusion, this introductory chapter sets the stage for a captivating exploration of how culture influences our most intimate and profound human experiences. As we embark on this journey, we invite readers to open their

INTRODUCTION

minds to the myriad ways in which love and marriage are shaped by the societies we inhabit. Through this exploration, we aspire to not only broaden our perspectives but also deepen our collective understanding of what it means to love and be loved in a world rich with cultural diversity.

2

Love Across Cultures

Love, often considered a universal emotion, manifests in remarkably diverse ways across cultures. This chapter delves into the multifaceted concept of love, exploring its manifestations and expressions through the lenses of different cultural viewpoints. We will examine how cultural norms, values, and traditions influence the understanding and demonstration of love, shedding light on the intricate interplay between individual emotions and collective beliefs.

2.1 The Universality and Diversity of Love

While the emotion of love is experienced across cultures, its interpretations and expressions vary significantly. Love can encompass romantic passion, familial bonds, platonic friendships, and spiritual connections, each of which may carry distinct cultural meanings. The universality of love is found in the emotional depth it offers, yet its cultural diversity emerges from the ways it is understood, communicated, and valued within societies.

2.2 Love as a Cultural Construct

Cultural norms play a pivotal role in shaping how love is perceived and enacted. In some cultures, arranged marriages are common, emphasizing the role of family and community in the union of two individuals. In contrast, societies that prioritize individual autonomy may celebrate romantic love as the foundation of marriage. These varying perspectives reflect cultural priorities and ideals, illustrating how love is intertwined with broader societal values.

2.3 Expressions of Affection

Expressions of love are deeply influenced by cultural context. In some cultures, physical touch and public displays of affection are encouraged, while in others, such actions might be considered inappropriate or reserved for private spaces. Similarly, verbal expressions of love, such as saying "I love you," carry distinct weight across cultures. Some languages and cultures have multiple words to capture different facets of love, emphasizing the richness of emotional experience.

2.4 Rituals and Traditions

Cultural traditions and rituals often provide a framework for the expression and celebration of love. Weddings, for example, are not only a union of individuals but also a merging of families and communities. The rituals surrounding weddings vary widely, from elaborate ceremonies to intimate gatherings, reflecting cultural values and priorities. These traditions shape not only the event itself but also the expectations and responsibilities within the marital relationship.

2.5 Influence of Media and Globalization

In an increasingly interconnected world, media and globalization have the power to shape cultural perceptions of love. Popular media, including movies, music, and literature, can reinforce or challenge cultural norms. The spread of globalized ideals of romance can lead to both the adoption of new perspectives and the preservation of traditional values, highlighting the dynamic interplay between local and global influences.

2.6 Challenges and Opportunities

While cultural diversity enriches our understanding of love, it can also pose challenges. Inter-cultural relationships may require navigating differences in communication styles, expectations, and values. However, these challenges also provide opportunities for personal growth, empathy, and the creation of new, inclusive cultural narratives.

In conclusion, this chapter has explored the complex landscape of love across cultures. By recognizing the ways in which cultural norms and values shape our understanding and expression of love, we gain a deeper appreciation for the intricate interplay between individual emotions and collective influences. As we proceed through this book, we invite readers to reflect on the diverse ways in which love is woven into the fabric of human existence, celebrating both its universality and its cultural diversity.

3

Traditional Marriage Customs

Marriage, a cornerstone of human society, is celebrated and solemnized through a myriad of customs and rituals across cultures. This chapter delves into the rich tapestry of traditional marriage customs, offering a glimpse into the diverse ways in which different societies mark the union of two individuals. By examining these rituals and practices, we uncover the profound symbolism and cultural significance that underlie marriage ceremonies worldwide.

3.1 Cultural Diversity in Marriage Customs

Marriage customs are deeply rooted in cultural traditions, reflecting the unique histories, values, and beliefs of each society. From the vibrant festivities of Indian weddings to the quiet solemnity of Japanese ceremonies, the rituals surrounding marriage are as diverse as the cultures that celebrate them. Exploring these customs allows us to witness the intricate ways in which love and commitment are expressed and celebrated around the world.

3.2 Symbolism in Rituals

Many marriage customs are laden with symbolism, each element contributing to the larger narrative of the union. For instance, the exchange of rings in Western weddings symbolizes eternal love and unity, while the use of henna in South Asian ceremonies signifies blessings and protection. These symbols connect the personal experience of the couple to the collective heritage of their culture, bridging the gap between individual desires and communal expectations.

3.3 Bridging Past and Present

Marriage customs often serve as a bridge between the past and the present, connecting generations and preserving cultural continuity. Rituals that have been passed down for centuries carry the weight of history, reminding participants of their roots and heritage. At the same time, modern adaptations of these customs reflect the evolving values and sensibilities of contemporary society.

3.4 Community and Family Involvement

Traditional marriage customs are frequently communal affairs, emphasizing the role of family and community in the union of two individuals. The involvement of parents, elders, and community leaders signifies not only their support for the couple but also the merging of families and the continuation of lineage. The rituals become a celebration not just of the couple's love, but of the bonds that connect broader networks of people.

3.5 Transition and Transformation

Marriage ceremonies often mark a significant life transition, signifying the shift from individual to couple, from daughter or son to spouse. These transitions are punctuated by rituals that symbolize leaving behind one stage of life and embarking on another. From the bittersweet farewells in some African cultures to the elaborate purification rituals in certain Middle

Eastern traditions, these customs embody the idea that marriage brings forth transformation and growth.

3.6 Adaptation in the Modern World

In the face of social change and globalization, traditional marriage customs have not remained stagnant. Many cultures are finding ways to preserve the essence of their customs while adapting to contemporary sensibilities. This highlights the resilience of cultural practices and their ability to evolve while maintaining their core significance.

In conclusion, this chapter has explored the intricate tapestry of traditional marriage customs from around the world. These customs serve as a lens through which we can understand the intersections of culture, love, and commitment. By studying the symbolism and significance of these rituals, we gain insights into the complex ways in which cultures celebrate and honor the institution of marriage, enriching our understanding of the human experience across diverse societies.

4

Arranged Marriages

Arranged marriages, a practice deeply rooted in tradition and culture, have been a significant aspect of marital unions in various societies across the globe. This chapter delves into the complexities, benefits, and challenges associated with arranged marriages, shedding light on the intricate interplay between individual choices and communal expectations.

4.1 Cultural Context and Diversity

Arranged marriages vary widely in form and function across cultures. In some societies, families play a central role in selecting potential partners, while in others, matchmakers or religious leaders facilitate the process. The reasons behind arranged marriages can range from maintaining family alliances and preserving cultural traditions to ensuring compatibility in terms of religion, caste, or social status.

4.2 Complexities of Choice and Consent

Arranged marriages raise questions about the balance between individual autonomy and societal pressures. While it might seem that choice and consent are compromised, it's important to recognize that consent can take on different forms in different cultural contexts. Often, the consent of families and the recognition of shared values play a significant role in the decision-making process.

4.3 Benefits of Arranged Marriages

Arranged marriages are often seen as a means of ensuring compatibility between partners. Families consider factors beyond immediate emotional attraction, such as shared values, financial stability, and social compatibility. This approach can lead to long-lasting unions built on a foundation of shared goals and values. Additionally, arranged marriages can strengthen social networks and reinforce community ties.

4.4 Challenges and Criticisms

Critics of arranged marriages highlight potential drawbacks, such as limited agency for the individuals involved and the risk of coercion. The emphasis on compatibility in areas like caste, religion, or socioeconomic status can perpetuate social inequalities. Moreover, the pressure to conform to societal norms can lead to suppressed individual desires and unfulfilled expectations.

4.5 Changing Dynamics

In an era of globalization and increased individualism, the dynamics of arranged marriages are evolving. Younger generations often seek a balance between tradition and personal agency. Arranged marriages today may involve greater communication between potential partners, allowing them to get to know each other and express their preferences before making a decision.

4.6 Success and Adaptation

The success of arranged marriages hinges on various factors, including the degree of agency afforded to the individuals, the level of communication between families and partners, and the cultural values that underpin the practice. When arranged marriages allow for flexibility, open communication, and mutual respect, they can thrive in a changing world.

4.7 Cultural Identity and Diversity

Arranged marriages showcase the complexities of cultural identity and the negotiation of tradition in a modern context. Some individuals choose to embrace the practice as a way of preserving their cultural heritage, while others may challenge or adapt it to align with their personal values.

In conclusion, this chapter has examined the intricate practice of arranged marriages in diverse cultural contexts. While the complexities, benefits, and challenges associated with arranged marriages are manifold, it's important to recognize that this practice is not monolithic. Arranged marriages underscore the constant negotiation between tradition and modernity, individual choice and collective expectations, providing us with valuable insights into the ways in which cultural practices shape human relationships.

5

Family and Community Involvement

The role of families and communities in relationships and marriages is a defining feature of many cultures. This chapter delves into the intricate dynamics of family and community involvement, examining how cultural collectivism shapes decisions, support systems, and the broader context of love and marriage.

5.1 The Collective Nature of Relationships

In cultures with strong family and community ties, relationships are not solely between two individuals; they extend to encompass families and networks of relatives. These close-knit structures foster a sense of belonging and interconnectedness, shaping the way individuals approach romantic relationships and marriages.

5.2 Family as Decision-Makers

In many societies, families play an active role in the decision-making process when it comes to relationships and marriages. Factors such as compatibility, social status, and shared values are considered not only for the individuals involved but also for the families they represent. This collective decision-making reflects the belief that unions impact the broader community.

5.3 Support Systems and Social Networks

Family and community involvement provides a robust support system for couples. Marriages are not only unions of two people but also unions of families, creating a web of support that spans generations. These support systems can provide emotional, financial, and practical assistance, contributing to the stability of relationships.

5.4 Preserving Cultural Traditions

The involvement of families and communities often stems from a desire to uphold cultural traditions and values. Marriages are seen as a means of continuing lineage, preserving heritage, and ensuring the continuation of cultural practices. Family and community engagement reinforces cultural identity and reinforces the importance of collective bonds.

5.5 Navigating Conflicting Expectations

While family and community involvement can provide a strong support network, it can also lead to conflicting expectations. Balancing personal desires with communal obligations can be challenging. The negotiation between individual autonomy and collective harmony requires careful communication and understanding.

5.6 Evolving Dynamics in Modern Contexts

In a rapidly changing world, the dynamics of family and community involvement are evolving. As societies become more globalized and individualistic, younger generations may seek greater agency in their relationships. Balancing tradition with personal aspirations requires open conversations and mutual respect.

5.7 Globalization and Cross-Cultural Marriages

Globalization has led to an increase in cross-cultural marriages, bringing together individuals from diverse backgrounds. These unions often require negotiating not only personal differences but also the expectations of multiple families and communities. Cross-cultural marriages highlight the need for understanding and flexibility in accommodating diverse viewpoints.

In conclusion, this chapter has explored the significant role of families and communities in relationships and marriages. Cultural collectivism shapes decision-making processes, support systems, and the broader context in which love and marriage unfold. While the complexities of balancing personal desires and communal expectations are evident, the involvement of families and communities also underscores the importance of interconnectedness and the preservation of cultural heritage. Understanding these dynamics enriches our appreciation for the intricate interplay between the individual and the collective within diverse societies.

6

Gender Roles and Expectations

Cultural expectations surrounding gender roles within relationships form a cornerstone of societies around the world. This chapter delves into the intricate ways in which cultural norms shape perceptions of gender and influence power dynamics, responsibilities, and interactions within marriages and partnerships.

6.1 Gender as a Cultural Construct

Gender roles are not universal but rather culturally constructed. Societies assign specific behaviors, roles, and expectations to individuals based on their perceived gender. These roles can influence everything from domestic responsibilities to decision-making processes within relationships.

6.2 Cultural Norms and Power Dynamics

Cultural norms often establish power dynamics within relationships. Some societies uphold traditional notions of male dominance and female submission, while others emphasize equality and partnership. These norms can impact decision-making, control over resources, and overall agency within relationships.

6.3 Division of Labor

Cultural norms influence how responsibilities are divided along gender lines. Household chores, childcare, and financial contributions may be distributed differently based on gender roles. These divisions can have implications for the distribution of power and influence within the relationship.

6.4 Influence on Communication Styles

Cultural expectations around gender roles can also shape communication styles. Societies that value assertiveness and directness may expect these traits from men, while women might be encouraged to display more nurturing and empathetic qualities. These differing communication styles can influence how couples express their needs and navigate conflicts.

6.5 Impact on Decision-Making

Gender norms often play a significant role in decision-making processes within relationships. In some cultures, men may be expected to make major decisions, while women's opinions may be valued more in matters related to the household. These dynamics can influence the sense of agency and autonomy of each partner.

6.6 Evolving Gender Roles

In many societies, gender roles are evolving as cultural norms adapt to changing social and economic landscapes. Women's empowerment movements and increased access to education and opportunities are challenging traditional gender norms, leading to shifts in power dynamics and expectations within relationships.

6.7 Intersectionality and Cultural Complexity

Gender roles do not exist in isolation; they intersect with other aspects of identity such as race, class, and sexuality. This intersectionality adds layers of complexity to cultural expectations. For example, the gender roles experienced by a woman in one culture may differ significantly from those experienced by a woman in another culture.

In conclusion, this chapter has explored the profound influence of cultural expectations surrounding gender roles within relationships. These norms shape power dynamics, division of labor, communication styles, and decision-making processes. Recognizing the impact of these expectations on the dynamics of relationships allows us to appreciate the complexities of navigating cultural norms while striving for equality and mutual respect. Understanding the intersections of gender and culture enriches our comprehension of the multifaceted nature of human relationships across diverse societies.

7

Love and Religion

Love and religion are two of the most powerful and enduring forces in the human experience. They have shaped cultures, influenced societies, and guided individuals for centuries. In this chapter, we will delve deep into the intricate relationship between love and religion, exploring how they intersect, influence one another, and impact our lives.

The Multifaceted Nature of Love

Love, in all its forms, is a universal human experience. It encompasses romantic love, familial love, platonic love, and love for humanity. It is a force that transcends borders, languages, and beliefs. When we examine love within the context of religion, we discover that it takes on unique and multifaceted dimensions.

In many religious traditions, love is seen as a divine gift, a reflection of the transcendent love of a higher power or deity. In Christianity, for example, God's love for humanity is a central theme. The Bible's famous verse, John 3:16, encapsulates this notion: "For God so loved the world that he gave his one and only Son, that whoever believes in him shall not perish but have eternal life." This divine love is believed to inspire and guide human love, encouraging compassion, forgiveness, and selflessness.

Love as a Path to the Divine

Across various religions, love is often considered a means of connecting with the divine. In Hinduism, the concept of "Bhakti" emphasizes devotion and love for a personal deity as a way to attain spiritual enlightenment. Devotees express their love through prayer, rituals, and acts of service, believing that their love for the divine deepens their understanding of the sacred.

In Sufi Islam, the mystical branch of the faith, love for God is central. Sufis speak of "ishq" or divine love, which is an intense, passionate love for the divine. They view their journey towards God as a journey of love, and poetry and music often play a role in expressing this profound affection. Rumi, the famous Sufi poet, beautifully captures this sentiment: "Let yourself be silently drawn by the strange pull of what you really love. It will not lead you astray."

Challenges of Love and Religion

While love and religion can harmoniously coexist, they can also present challenges. Interfaith relationships, for example, require individuals to navigate differences in belief systems and practices. Such relationships can be a test of tolerance, understanding, and compromise.

Similarly, societal and cultural norms often influence the expression of love. In some communities, love marriages may be discouraged or even forbidden, with arranged marriages being the preferred route. In these cases, love and religious or cultural expectations may come into conflict, highlighting the complexity of this relationship.

Love's Capacity for Healing and Unity

Love has an extraordinary capacity to heal divisions, foster unity, and bridge religious and cultural gaps. Interfaith dialogue and cooperation have been on the rise, with individuals from different religious backgrounds coming together to work on common causes, such as humanitarian efforts, social justice, and environmental conservation.

Moreover, the principles of love, compassion, and empathy that are often central to religious teachings can serve as common ground for people of diverse faiths. In times of crisis, love and compassion have a unifying effect, transcending religious boundaries to bring communities together.

In conclusion, the intersection of love and religion is a rich and complex tapestry. While it can present challenges, it also holds the potential for profound spiritual growth, unity, and the creation of a more compassionate and interconnected world. Whether expressed through devotion to a higher power or through acts of kindness and understanding toward fellow human beings, the relationship between love and religion remains a powerful and enduring aspect of the human experience.

8

Celebrating Milestones and Anniversaries

The celebration of relationship milestones and anniversaries is a universal practice that takes on unique cultural flavors. This chapter delves into the diverse ways in which cultures mark significant moments within relationships and examines the profound meanings attached to these celebrations.

8.1 Cultural Variations in Celebration

Across cultures, the ways in which relationship milestones are celebrated can vary greatly. From elaborate ceremonies to intimate gatherings, these celebrations reflect cultural values, traditions, and expectations. The diversity in these practices illustrates the rich tapestry of human relationships around the world.

8.2 Marking Marriage Anniversaries

Marriage anniversaries are perhaps the most universally recognized milestones. Different cultures have their own traditions for commemorating these occasions. While some may involve lavish parties and gift exchanges, others might emphasize quiet reflection and reaffirmation of vows. Regardless of the approach, these anniversaries provide couples with an opportunity to reflect on their journey and reaffirm their commitment.

8.3 Cultural Significance

The cultural significance of celebrating relationship milestones extends beyond the couple involved. These celebrations often serve as affirmations of the broader community's support and validation of the relationship. The involvement of family and friends reinforces the idea that the union is not just between two individuals but also between families and communities.

8.4 Rituals and Symbolism

Rituals and symbolism play a central role in celebrating milestones. In some cultures, couples might partake in rituals that symbolize renewal and transformation. For instance, exchanging new rings or clothing can symbolize the continuous growth of love. These rituals reinforce the deeper meanings associated with these milestones.

8.5 Strengthening Bonds

Celebrating milestones provides an opportunity for couples to strengthen their emotional bonds. The act of coming together, sharing stories, and reaffirming vows fosters a sense of connection and intimacy. These celebrations offer a reminder of the journey the couple has undertaken and the challenges they have overcome together.

8.6 Influence of Tradition and Modernity

In an era of rapid change, the celebration of relationship milestones is also evolving. While traditional customs hold significance, modern couples may choose to adapt these practices to align with their personal values and preferences. The blending of tradition and modernity showcases the resilience of cultural practices in a changing world.

8.7 Cross-Cultural Celebrations

Cross-cultural relationships often lead to the fusion of various celebration practices. Partners from different backgrounds may choose to incorporate elements from each other's traditions, creating hybrid celebrations that honor their shared and individual identities.

In conclusion, this chapter has explored the diverse ways in which cultures celebrate relationship milestones and anniversaries. These celebrations are a testament to the enduring power of love, connection, and community. By examining the rituals, symbolism, and cultural meanings attached to these occasions, we gain insights into the universal human desire to mark and honor the milestones of our relationships.

9

Relationship Dynamics in Changing Times

Cultural perspectives on love and marriage are not static; they evolve over generations in response to changing societal norms, globalization, and modernization. This chapter delves into the ways in which cultural views on relationships are shifting and examines the impact of these changes on traditional practices.

9.1 Evolving Views on Love and Marriage

Cultural perspectives on love and marriage are influenced by historical contexts, social progress, and generational shifts. As societies evolve, so do the values and expectations attached to relationships. Younger generations often approach love and marriage with different priorities and sensibilities compared to their predecessors.

9.2 Impact of Social Change

Social change plays a pivotal role in shaping evolving cultural perspectives.

Movements advocating for gender equality, LGBTQ+ rights, and individual autonomy are challenging traditional norms and prompting reevaluations of relationship dynamics. These changes reflect broader shifts in societal values and attitudes.

9.3 Globalization's Influence

Globalization has exposed individuals to a plethora of cultural viewpoints on relationships through media, travel, and intercultural interactions. This exposure can lead to the adoption of new ideas while also fostering a sense of cultural pride and identity preservation. Globalization contributes to the blurring of cultural boundaries and the sharing of diverse relationship models.

9.4 Modernization and Technology

Advancements in technology have revolutionized the way individuals form and maintain relationships. Online dating, social media, and communication platforms have altered the way people connect, bridging geographical distances and introducing new avenues for meeting potential partners. These technological shifts impact cultural practices by providing individuals with greater agency in their relationships.

9.5 Navigating Tradition and Modernity

Many cultures are navigating the delicate balance between tradition and modernity. Younger generations often seek to preserve cultural heritage while adapting to contemporary values. This can result in hybrid practices that blend traditional rituals with modern sensibilities, reflecting the dynamic nature of cultural perspectives.

9.6 Impact on Family Dynamics

Evolving cultural perspectives on love and marriage have ripple effects on family dynamics. As younger generations assert their individual choices, familial expectations may need to be renegotiated. Open conversations and mutual understanding become crucial in bridging the gaps between generations.

9.7 Celebrating Diversity

The evolving nature of cultural perspectives on relationships underscores the importance of celebrating diversity. As societies become more multicultural, there is an opportunity to learn from different viewpoints and embrace the richness of human experience. Acknowledging these differences fosters greater empathy and understanding.

In conclusion, this chapter has explored the fluid nature of cultural perspectives on love and marriage in response to changing times. The impact of social change, globalization, and modernization shapes how individuals approach relationships and influences the preservation or transformation of traditional practices. By recognizing these shifts, we gain insights into the adaptive nature of culture and the enduring quest to navigate the complexities of human relationships in a rapidly changing world.

10

Cross-Cultural Relationships

Cross-cultural relationships, often characterized by the union of individuals from diverse cultural backgrounds, offer both unique challenges and profound opportunities for growth. This chapter delves into the complexities and benefits of such relationships, providing insights into how cultural differences can be navigated and mutual understanding fostered.

10.1 Embracing Diversity

Cross-cultural relationships celebrate the beauty of diversity, as individuals from different cultural backgrounds come together to form connections. These relationships challenge preconceived notions, broaden perspectives, and allow couples to experience the richness of multiple cultures.

10.2 Navigating Cultural Differences

Cultural differences can lead to misunderstandings and conflicts, stemming from varying communication styles, expectations, and values. The key lies in recognizing that these differences are neither inherently good nor bad, but rather reflect the diverse ways in which people interpret the world. Open dialogue and mutual respect are essential for navigating these challenges.

10.3 Benefits of Exposure

Cross-cultural relationships provide opportunities for personal growth and learning. Experiencing another culture firsthand can lead to increased empathy, adaptability, and a broader worldview. Individuals in these relationships often gain insights into their own cultural biases and expand their horizons through exposure to new traditions and beliefs.

10.4 Shared Identity

Cross-cultural couples often develop a unique shared identity that transcends cultural boundaries. They may create their own rituals, communication styles, and ways of navigating challenges, drawing from the best of both worlds. This shared identity fosters a sense of unity that encompasses their individual backgrounds.

10.5 Balancing Traditions

One challenge in cross-cultural relationships is striking a balance between preserving one's own cultural traditions and integrating those of a partner. Flexibility, compromise, and willingness to learn about and participate in each other's traditions can create a harmonious blend of cultural practices.

10.6 Strengthening Communication

Effective communication is paramount in cross-cultural relationships. Partners must navigate nuances in language, tone, and nonverbal cues to ensure that messages are accurately understood. Learning to communicate openly, while being attuned to cultural sensitivities, enhances mutual understanding.

10.7 Seeking Common Values

While cultures may have different traditions, they often share common human values such as respect, love, and compassion. Recognizing these shared values can serve as a bridge, helping partners find common ground and align their goals and aspirations.

10.8 Support and Resources

Cross-cultural couples can benefit from seeking support through counseling, cultural sensitivity workshops, and connecting with others in similar relationships. These resources provide tools for addressing challenges and fostering a deeper understanding of each other's backgrounds.

In conclusion, this chapter has explored the intricate dynamics of cross-cultural relationships. These relationships offer the opportunity to celebrate diversity, challenge assumptions, and embrace new perspectives. By navigating the complexities of cultural differences with open communication, mutual respect, and a willingness to learn, cross-cultural couples can forge strong, resilient partnerships that enrich their lives and contribute to the broader tapestry of human relationships.

11

Conflict Resolution Across Cultures

Conflict is an inevitable part of any relationship, and the ways in which conflicts are resolved can vary significantly across cultures. This chapter delves into the diverse approaches to conflict resolution within relationships, examining how cultural communication styles and strategies influence the resolution process.

11.1 Cultural Influences on Conflict Perception

Cultural norms shape how individuals perceive and respond to conflicts. Some cultures prioritize open confrontation and direct communication, while others value harmony and avoid confrontations that might disrupt relationships. Understanding these cultural nuances is crucial for effective conflict resolution.

11.2 Communication Styles

Cultural differences in communication styles impact how conflicts are addressed. Some cultures emphasize explicit communication, where individuals voice their opinions and feelings directly. Others may prefer indirect communication, relying on nonverbal cues and context to convey messages. Misunderstandings can arise when partners have different communication preferences.

11.3 Conflict Avoidance vs. Confrontation

Cultural norms often determine whether conflict is addressed head-on or avoided. Some cultures view confrontation as healthy for relationship growth, while others emphasize the importance of maintaining harmony even if it means avoiding disagreements. These differing approaches can lead to tensions when partners have conflicting expectations.

11.4 Collectivism vs. Individualism

Cultural collectivism and individualism influence how conflicts are perceived within relationships. In collectivist cultures, individuals may prioritize the needs of the group and downplay personal grievances. In individualistic cultures, personal needs and opinions might take precedence. Understanding these dynamics helps partners empathize with each other's perspectives.

11.5 Strategies for Resolution

Cultural norms also influence the strategies used for conflict resolution. Some cultures value compromise and finding middle ground, while others prioritize asserting one's position. Collaborative problem-solving and active listening are universally valuable tools, but their implementation might differ based on cultural context.

11.6 Role of Elders and Mediators

In some cultures, conflicts within relationships are resolved with the involvement of elders or respected community members who act as mediators. These figures bring wisdom and neutral perspectives, facilitating open dialogue and negotiation.

11.7 Embracing Diversity in Resolution Styles

Partners from different cultural backgrounds can learn from each other's conflict resolution styles. Embracing the strengths of diverse approaches can lead to a more comprehensive toolkit for addressing conflicts and cultivating healthier relationships.

11.8 Building a Common Approach

Cross-cultural couples can benefit from developing a conflict resolution approach that draws from both partners' cultural backgrounds. This collaborative strategy allows for mutual understanding, compromises, and a shared sense of emotional safety.

In conclusion, this chapter has explored the intricate interplay between cultural perspectives and conflict resolution within relationships. Understanding how communication styles, approaches to confrontation, and values surrounding harmony differ across cultures is essential for fostering effective conflict resolution. By recognizing and valuing these cultural nuances, couples can navigate conflicts with greater empathy, mutual respect, and a deeper appreciation for the diversity that enriches their relationships.

12

Celebrating Diversity and Unity

As we reach the conclusion of this exploration into the cultural perspectives on love and marriage, we are reminded of the wealth of insights that arise from embracing the diverse ways in which different societies approach these fundamental aspects of human relationships. This final chapter reflects on the journey we've undertaken and encapsulates the key takeaways, encouraging readers to celebrate and embrace cultural diversity in their own relationships.

12.1 Embracing Cultural Diversity

Throughout this book, we've journeyed through a tapestry of cultural viewpoints, traditions, and practices surrounding love and marriage. We've explored how cultural norms shape everything from expressions of affection and relationship milestones to conflict resolution strategies. By celebrating cultural diversity, we open ourselves to a deeper understanding of the myriad ways in which humans experience and express love.

12.2 Key Takeaways

- **Cultural Complexity**: Our exploration has highlighted the complex interplay between tradition and modernity, individual desires and communal expectations. Cultural norms are not fixed; they evolve and adapt over time.

- **Communication and Understanding**: Effective communication and empathy are paramount in navigating the nuances of cultural perspectives. Open dialogue and a willingness to learn from each other foster mutual understanding.

- **Balancing Tradition and Autonomy**: Many cultures navigate the balance between preserving cultural traditions and embracing personal autonomy. Partners can find common ground by honoring their heritage while creating a shared path forward.

- **Conflict and Resolution**: Cultural approaches to conflict resolution vary widely. Recognizing these differences and finding common strategies can lead to healthier relationships.

- **Globalization's Impact**: Globalization has exposed us to a plethora of cultural viewpoints. It has also encouraged the preservation of cultural identity while fostering cross-cultural connections.

12.3 Celebrating Unity in Diversity

As we celebrate the unity that love and marriage bring to our lives, we must also celebrate the diversity that enriches our understanding of these experiences. Just as individuals from different cultures come together in relationships, we too can create a harmonious blend of perspectives that enrich our lives.

12.4 Moving Forward

As readers, you are invited to carry the insights gained from this exploration into your own lives and relationships. Whether you are in a cross-cultural partnership or simply seeking to broaden your cultural horizons, embracing diversity can lead to deeper connections, greater empathy, and a more profound appreciation for the multifaceted nature of human relationships.

In conclusion, this book has taken us on a journey through the landscapes of love and marriage, exploring the ways in which culture influences our understanding, expressions, and experiences. The cultural tapestry we've woven together demonstrates that while love is universal, its manifestations are beautifully diverse. Let us move forward with open hearts and minds, celebrating the unity in diversity that defines the rich human experience.

www.ingramcontent.com/pod-product-compliance
Lightning Source LLC
LaVergne TN
LVHW020739090526
838202LV00057BA/5990